HARMONY

A GUIDE TO EMOTIONAL WELL-BEING

AID ASSOCIATION FOR LUTHERANS

11710 9-94

CONTENTS

INTRODUCTION

Harmony of the mind, body and spirit. Everyone wants it. It's a harmony that God intends for all of creation.

But harmony can be disrupted by the stresses of life—strained relationships, illnesses, failed hopes, broken promises, and lives shattered by job loss, divorce, and death.

The wonder is that harmony of mind, body and spirit remains God's gracious gift to us, no matter how severe the stresses and strains of life. It is a gift of God's continuing creation, and everyone of us can receive it.

We all face daily challenges to our emotional well-being as we journey through life. Many of these challenges are really only minor inconveniences—like locking our keys in our car. Others are more serious—like a breakdown on an unfamiliar road.

Some of us manage these daily challenges, these stressors, very well. But many of us could react to our problems, whether they are minor frustrations or deep sorrows, in a healthier way. The good news is that we can begin to respond better to the stress in our lives by making *small changes*. Then, as we feel the difference these changes make, we'll become encouraged to try

new things to lessen our stress. We may change our diet and start an exercise program, practice relaxation techniques, or read scripture and meditate in an effort to become more spiritually grounded. These small and then larger steps give us our forward motion, leading us toward harmony and health.

This book guides you through these steps to help you find harmony of mind, body and spirit. It makes you an active participant in finding strategies to meet and lessen the stressors that are part of life.

There are exercises throughout the book designed to help you identify what's right for you personally in the individual challenges you face. Some of these exercises may seem difficult, especially at first, but if you try even a few of them, you'll find they can lead to better physical, emotional, and spiritual health in your life. You're invited to write your thoughts in the spaces provided within the exercises and also at the end of the book in the "Notes" pages.

Your responses throughout the book will outline some of the most important and most basic steps you can take to gain perspective in your life and improve your emotional well-being.

Understanding How Stress Works

Stress is both physiological and emotional. It's your reaction to the demands that are placed upon you.

Whether it's the paycheck that doesn't quite cover monthly expenses, the young children who clamor for attention when we're tired, the bus we just missed, the job we're in danger of losing, or a parent's chronic illness, no one is spared from daily stress, large or small. Day-to-day stress is a common physical and mental challenge for all of us.

There are certain things you can do to ensure a less stressful passage through life. But first, it helps to understand how stress works.

> It's our reaction to problems, more than the problems themselves, that has the greatest impact on our personal well-being.
>
> ◆

List below the things you worry about on a regular basis—housework, bills, health, job security and so on.

Study this list and circle the ones you *can* control.

_____

_____

_____

_____

_____

_____

_____

_____

_____

_____

_____

_____

What does this tell you about worries that sap your time and energy?

HOW WE WEAR OURSELVES OUT

In the 1930s, Hans Selye, M.D., became the first scientist to study the body's response to stress. Selye defined stress as simply "the rate of wear and tear on the body." He studied the adaptation that takes place in our bodies when we are faced with a change, whether that change is physical (temperature or chemical irritants in the air) or emotional (anger or joy).

Indeed, one of the most interesting and frustrating aspects of stress is the number of different situations that can produce it. Fear, anger, failure, a promotion, birth of a child—each of these can produce a degree of stress in any person. No single action can be identified as the cause of stress. Selye did find, though, that the pattern of *reaction* to any of these causes was the same.

The physical manifestations of stress became the basis for developing the stress concept: When we're under stress, certain hormones kick in. Blood is pumped faster. Oxygen is delivered more quickly to the brain. Blood sugar rises, and fat stores are broken down to provide extra energy. This allows us to respond quickly, to answer sharply. In other words, stress can give us the immediate lift and energy we need to handle a challenge and it can wear us out.

Even stress that is helpful is tiring. That's why we sometimes feel worn out after a wedding, vacation, or delivering a great speech. Selye found that no amount of

sleep and rest after such an episode can completely restore our levels of resistance. He also found that the physiological responses chronic stress causes are much more than is needed to manage many of the small and constant pressures we encounter. Clearly, it makes sense to monitor and lessen the stress in our lives that draws from the finite amount of stress resistence within each of us.

Often, it's our *perception* of events that makes them stressful. The way we *think* about events, not the events themselves, causes us to *feel* stressed.

Imagine a group of children happily climbing on playground equipment at the neighborhood park. Their parents are sitting around talking in a relaxed manner, helping their children when they need it. Except for one mom. She hovers over her child at the swing, slide, and jungle gym. She reads danger into everything about the situation. By feeling that way, she's causing herself unnecessary stress.

Praying the serenity prayer can help us gain perspective:

"Lord, grant me the serenity to accept the things I cannot change; the courage to change the things I can; and the wisdom to know the difference."

Reinhold Neibuhr

KNOW THE SIGNS OF STRESS

Before we can learn to control our stress, we must assess how much stress we have and what in our lives contributes most to it. Then we can concentrate on making changes where we're able and learn to accept those situations where we can't.

Physical signs that indicate stress might include: Sleeping troubles, headaches, nail biting, breathlessness, fainting or dizzy spells, crying often or wishing to, high blood pressure, an inclination to take an alcoholic drink to relax, or smoking to calm yourself.

Mental signs that indicate stress might include: feeling unable to cope; general irritability; feeling as if you have failed yourself, your spouse, or children; indecision; or difficulty concentrating on or finishing a project.

The stress test that follows will give you a more complete picture of your physical and mental stress levels.

How do you cope with stress?*
A Self-Report Checklist Designed for Health Education Purposes

This is a health education survey, not a clinical assessment instrument. Its sole purpose is to inform you of how you cope with the stress in your life.

Directions: Simply follow the instructions given for each of the 14 items listed below. When you have completed all of the 14 items, place your total score in the space provided.

_____ 1. Give yourself 10 points if you feel that you have a supportive family.

_____ 2. Give yourself 10 points if you actively pursue a hobby.

_____ 3. Give yourself 10 points if you belong to some social or activity group that meets at least once a month (other than your family).

_____ 4. Give yourself 15 points if you are within five pounds of your "ideal" bodyweight, considering your height and bone structure.

_____ 5. Give yourself 15 points if you practice some form of "deep relaxation" at least three times a week. Deep relaxation exercises include spiritual meditation, deep breathing, and slow stretching.

_____ 6. Give yourself 5 points for each time you exercise 30 minutes or longer during the course of an average week.

_____ 7. Give yourself 5 points for each nutritionally balanced and wholesome meal you consume during the course of an average day.

____ 8. Give yourself 5 points for each time you do something that you really enjoy, "just for yourself," during the course of an average week.

____ 9. Give yourself 10 points if you have some place in your home that you can go to in order to relax and/or be by yourself.

____ 10. Give yourself 10 points if you practice time-management techniques in your daily life.

____ 11. Subtract 10 points for each pack of cigarettes you smoke during the course of an average day.

____ 12. Subtract 5 points for each evening during the course of an average week that you take any form of medication or chemical substance (including alcohol) to help you sleep.

____ 13. Subtract 10 points for each day during the course of an average week that you consume any form of medication or chemical substance (including alcohol) to reduce your anxiety or just calm you down.

____ 14. Subtract 5 points for each evening during the course of an average week that you bring work home; work that was meant to be done at your place of employment.

_____ **Total score**

After you've calculated your total score, consider that the higher your score, the greater your health-promoting coping practices. A "perfect" score would be around 115. Scores in the 50-60 range are probably adequate to cope with most common sources of stress.

Also keep in mind that items 1-10 represent health-promoting strategies, and items 11-14 represent maladaptive, health-eroding strategies. These maladaptive strategies are self-sustaining because they do provide at least some temporary relief from stress. In the long run, however, they serve to erode one's health. Ideally, health-promoting coping strategies (items 1-10) are the best to integrate into your lifestyle and will ultimately prove to be an effective preventive program against excessive stress.

*This test was originally developed for the U.S. Department of Health and Human Services National Health Fair by Dr. George S. Everly, Jr., Union Memorial Hospital, Baltimore, Maryland.

If you're plagued
with chronic stress,
consider talking with
a professional—
a counselor or therapist
who can help you
get to the root causes
of your stress.

◆

Pay attention to the connection between what you eat and how you feel. Do you feel edgy after drinking two cups of coffee in the morning? Tired an hour after eating an empty calorie snack? Keep a log here of food, drinks and feelings.

MORNING
What I eat and drink: _____

_____

Physical feeling: _____

_____

AFTERNOON
What I eat and drink: _____

_____

Physical feeling: _____

_____

EVENING
What I eat and drink: _____

_____

Physical feeling: _____

_____

Noticing these connections will make it easier to change unhealthy eating habits.

TAKE A BALANCED APPROACH TO MANAGING STRESS

Living a healthy lifestyle helps you to deal with stressful situations. Strategies to reduce your levels of stress include (but are not limited to) paying attention to what you eat, getting regular exercise, controlling your breathing, learning to relax, getting a good night's sleep, and rethinking your relationship with others.

Maintain a Healthy Eating Plan

A well-nourished body handles stress better. Many of us know the general guidelines for healthy eating:

♦ Low fat and sugar.

♦ High complex carbohydrates.

♦ Plenty of fresh fruits and vegetables.

We should also go easy on stimulants such as coffee and other drinks that contain caffeine.

Exercise Your Whole Body

Exercise has both physical and emotional benefits. It provides an outlet for tension and stress and helps limit them in the future.

Anyone, any age, and in any physical condition can enjoy the benefits and fun of an exercise program. You don't have to be eighteen and in peak condition to walk into a gym or dive into a pool. But if you are over 40 and haven't been involved in a regular exercise program for some time, or if you have a specific illness or physical restriction, you should consult your health care provider before beginning an exercise routine. Most people can begin a program of moderate exercise, such as brisk walking for thirty to forty minutes nearly every day, and feel the benefits almost immediately.

Walking also gives you the added benefit of enjoying the trees and the fresh air and maybe even noticing something new about the place you live.

You needn't be dependent on the weather for your walk. Many shopping malls open early in the morning to accommodate winter or bad weather walkers. Some malls even have regular walking clubs, which may be a good way to add a social aspect to your exercise routine.

Or you may choose to swim, run, bike, row, or skip rope. Whatever exercise you choose, remember to stretch before and after. This helps prevent muscle strains and pulls, and enhances the feeling of relaxation that will result from your physical efforts.

What kind of exercise can you do that is the equivalent of thirty minutes of brisk walking?

_____

What time of day is best for you to do it?

_____

How much time can you devote to it?

_____

Would you enjoy a class or group exercise situation, or would you rather it be a quiet time alone?

_____

_____

If you tailor your exercise routine to fit your personality, you'll be more likely to do it regularly.

_____

_____

_____

Which muscle group holds most of your tension?

_____

_____

What time of day do you typically feel most tense?

_____

_____

Can you set aside five minutes a day at that time to practice these techniques?

_____

Tell family members or friends that you are going to do this. (A public commitment to practicing relaxation techniques may make you more likely to do it.)

Relax and Let Go

Practicing muscle relaxation is another stress-reducing exercise that most of us can perform easily. And you don't need a lot of time or equipment to do it.

This exercise can help us increase our general body awareness and learn where we typically store our tension. The idea is to experience and note the difference in alternately tensing and relaxing specific muscle groups including not only the face, neck, and

shoulders (which often carry the brunt of our tension), but also the arms, hands, chest, back, legs, and feet. The basic technique is simple. It involves separately tensing your individual muscle groups, holding the tension for about five seconds, releasing the tension slowly while telling yourself to relax, and then taking a deep breath that you let out slowly, again telling yourself to relax.

Take a Deep Breath

Deep, slow, abdominal breathing is one of the most basic ways to cope with stress. But most of us don't automatically breathe in this manner.

Practice these steps to perfect the method:

1) Inhale deeply through your nose (your abdomen should rise, thus ensuring that you are using your diaphragm correctly).

2) Count to three or four as you fill your lungs.

3) Pause for a second before you exhale slowly through your nose, counting as you breathe out (try to exhale a count longer than you inhaled).

4) If the three or four count isn't comfortable at first, stop at two—don't strain, but work on extending the count.

5) Continue this breathing pattern fifteen to twenty times, but even three times will begin to slow your heart rate.

You can do this in bed when you're trying to doze off to sleep or you can do it even at the office. When you've finished this exercise, don't rush off to another task. Stay still, relaxed, for a minute or two. This deep breathing exercise is a good introduction to spiritual ways of handling stress, as are prayer and meditation.

Practice deep breathing at least once a day for a week, even if you don't think you need it. At the end of the week, write down any benefits you feel from it.

_____

_____

_____

_____

_____

_____

_____

Would it be useful to make this exercise part of your daily routine?

_____

_____

_____

_____

How often do you lie awake at night?

_____

_____

_____

What calming activities could you add to your nightly routine?

_____

_____

_____

_____

_____

_____

_____

Remember, insomnia and stress feed each other.

Managing Stress in Specific Situations

Most of us have experienced the stress that comes from insomnia and minor conflicts or frustrations with people we run into every day. But we do have a choice in how we react to these situations. The methods described on previous pages—diet, exercise, muscle relaxation, and proper breathing—are tools that can help us manage the stress of common daily challenges.

In addition, there are steps we can take to help us deal with a specific situational stressor, like insomnia.

It's when we need sleep most—when we are most stressed—that many of us have difficulty sleeping. Unlike wakefulness, sleep can't be forced. But often we try to do just that, making the problem even worse.

We can do things to increase our chances of falling asleep though. Exercising during the day, eating a light dinner, stretching lightly, doing only calming activities before going to bed (writing a letter or in your journal,

or reading), and limiting alcohol intake, can help ensure healthy sleeping patterns. Occasional sleep problems are common, especially when they occur during times of high stress. But if insomnia becomes a chronic problem, consult your physician.

Another common stressor is dealing with people on a daily basis.

We all have a choice about the impact we make on each other every day. This is true in "big" issues, such as how we vote on education funding or anti-discrimination legislation, and in the smaller daily choices we make, such as how we drive in heavy traffic or how we treat each other in the check-out line at the grocery store. We can add to the conflict or we can opt for peace of mind—for ourselves and our neighbors.

> The best plan for managing stress includes many parts in balance. When we become obsessive about managing or reducing our stress, we only add to the problem.
>
> ◆

Think of places you encounter people each day. How do you currently approach those people?

_____

_____

_____

_____

_____

What kind of response might come back to you if you greeted them with a smile?

_____

_____

_____

_____

_____

When Life
Brings Stress

When we enter a new, unknown phase of life, though we may be excited by the possibilities it offers, we worry about the outcome. Will we be a good parent? Should we take early retirement? As we enter phases of exceptional stress—phases that we know are deeply rooted in sadness and tragedy—the questions and anxieties hit us even harder. How can we help our terminally ill spouse? How do we talk to our children about divorce? Will we ever find a new job now that we've been laid off?

Once we settle into a new phase, even a particularly trying one, we adapt to it. The stress points come in anticipation of the change, the early phase of adjustment to it, or with the sudden onset of problems. But there are things we can do in every life stage to make our passage easier and to draw a little less from our finite store of stress resistance.

We stay healthier
when we take an active
role in our destiny.
This is true whether
we're nineteen
or ninety.

◆

19

Which life stage are you in?

_____

_____

What extra life pressures do you feel at this stage?

_____

_____

_____

_____

Which pressures have you handled well and which are you less satisfied with?

_____

_____

_____

_____

What can you learn from your reactions in the first case that will help you handle future life cycle stressors?

_____

_____

_____

_____

DEALING WITH STRESS IN DIFFERENT STAGES OF LIFE

Because change is the root of stress, any life changes may cause us stress. Marriage, parenting (especially parenting teens), middle age, and older age are some of the natural life cycles that bring stress to our lives.

Help Your Teenager Become Independent of You

We don't have to embrace our teenagers' everyday rebellions, but we should recognize the most superficial of them for what they are: Attempts, albeit misguided, to gain independence. During adolescence, children begin an earnest search to become who they want to be and to separate from their parents. They are constantly testing and pushing limits. If we recognize this, we'll be able to accept our son's earring and daughter's purple hair for what it is—a step toward independence—and not a personal attack on our values.

Sometimes kids can seem to challenge our values, while at the same time hoping we'll impose those values anyway. Most teenagers welcome the opportunity to blame parents when they aren't allowed to do something that pushed the limits further than they wanted to go. In these cases, we should willingly accept the role of "bad cop" to let our children off the hook with their friends. It may be very stressful to us at the time, but it's important to our kids.

Parents who listen actively and respectfully to their teens can exert great positive influence during years when it seems like every day holds a skirmish. Accepting that our teens are struggling to gain independence can help reduce family stress. Perhaps most important, we have to show love when our teens have done wrong, whatever that may be for a particular family.

Take an interest in your teenager's friends. What are their names?

_____

_____

_____

Their interests?

_____

_____

_____

What do you know about their families?

_____

_____

_____

_____

_____

Knowing something about your teen's friends gives you a patch of common ground, and it helps keep you aware of what your teen is thinking and doing.

Have you often said "I should volunteer at..." or "I should take a class in..." List some of those places and ideas here. Make a phone call today and take the first step toward pursuing your interests and meeting others in the process.

_____

_____

_____

_____

_____

_____

_____

_____

There is no break on internal and external stressors as children move out of adolescence and into young adulthood. At this stage, some of the key challenges for them are linked to being single, being a newlywed, or being a new parent.

Let a Permanent Relationship Evolve Naturally

Emotionally healthy single people don't make finding life partners their number one priority. Instead, these people work toward becoming more involved and well-rounded, pursuing interests and friendships, and developing the spiritual side of their lives. Ironically, people often find themselves developing permanent relationships *after* they stop making that a goal.

When we do date, we should be honest about what we want out of the relationship so that we don't set up false expectations and invite stress into our lives. If *he* wants a commitment, and *she* wants to meet and date lots of people, then *they* should work on developing a solid friendship instead of a romantic relationship.

Solve Problems Together with Your Spouse

If we do decide to marry, we should approach it realistically (while allowing ourselves plenty of time to bask in the corresponding romance).

Indeed, one of the keys to a successful marriage is joint problem solving. Though money, sex, and children are

often mentioned as the three most common problems in a marriage, how these differences are handled is usually much more important than the problem itself, especially during the early years. A couple that improves its communication skills before marrying is less likely to divorce. And even a couple in conflict can keep their relationship strong if they remember to show humor and affection toward each other.

When can you set aside time to sit down and really talk to your spouse?

_____

_____

_____

_____

_____

_____

Write it on your calendar. Think of it as an important commitment that you cannot miss.

And Baby Makes Three

At no time are men and women more susceptible to the stress of getting along with one another than when a baby is born. This tension comes at a time when a couple feels alternately exhilarated by their good fortune and physically and emotionally exhausted from lack of sleep due to taking care of a baby's needs and demands. Couples who share expectations and who talk to each other about their hopes, wishes, fears, and disappointments will be better parents and spouses. They may be so exhausted they fall asleep while talking, but it's important to make the effort.

List a few small things you could do today that would make your spouse's day a little easier.

_____

_____

_____

_____

_____

_____

_____

_____

_____

_____

Now, do one.

Plan the Rest of Your Life Together—Appreciate Middle Age

As we mature as adults, we're often left with a marriage that disturbs us because it seems commonplace and permanent. What happened to all of our dreams? The pressures of work, children, mortgage payments, and in-laws may leave a couple asking, "Is that all there is?"

The first and best thing to do when we feel this way is to confess the feeling to our spouse. It sounds obvious, but it's surprising how many people are afraid to do this. Once you're talking, it helps to work toward concrete goals that will improve your marriage such as handling the kids' carpool or sharing cooking and cleaning responsibilities.

Investing in the Family

Sometimes it seems as if we're missing the big picture in our relationships with our children. We spend so much time worrying about where they'll go to college, whether they're flunking math, and how quickly they're going to grow out of the expensive sneakers we just bought them, that we forget how much fun they can be.

Getting lost in our families is one of the deepest pleasures of our lives and it can also be a great way to relieve the stress and pressure we sometimes feel at work.

Write down at least one enjoyable thing you did with your family in the last month.

_____

_____

_____

_____

_____

_____

Now write down one enjoyable thing your family can do next month. Start planning now to make it happen.

_____

_____

_____

_____

_____

_____

_____

Take Pride in Doing the Best You Can While on the Job

Most of us have little real control over what happens to us in the workplace. The layoffs, restructuring, and "rightsizing" that have cost many first-rate workers their jobs in the past few years are testimony to this. Sometimes the best we can do is to isolate the parts of our job that we do have control over, set realistic deadlines for ourselves, meet these deadlines, and enjoy the sense of satisfaction and accomplishment we feel.

Middle age can also be a time of great opportunity in finding a new career. When we lose a job at this stage, we have enough workplace experience to make an honest estimation of whether we *want* to continue in the same profession. Many people in their thirties, forties, or fifties take advantage of a layoff or job loss to go back to school for additional training in their current career or to jump to a different career track.

Take Advantage of the Advantages of Maturity

The hard realities of aging include a menu of physical and emotional stressors that can tax the most able individuals. Two of the most common of these are the

potential need to move out of a home we've lived in for a long time and the grief we experience as we watch our friends and siblings die.

But the benefits of aging, including the perspective it bestows upon us naturally, can outweigh the sadness that it sometimes brings. In 1872, when she was sixty-seven, the writer George Sand explained this phenomenon: "You'll say the bark of the tree still has to bear the ravages of time. I don't mind that—the core is sound and the sap goes on doing its work, as in the old apple trees in my garden; the more gnarled they grow the more fruit they bear." Indeed, our mature faith, our increased ability to care about others, and the sure-footedness that comes with a lifetime of experience can make our years of older age particularly rewarding.

If living alone has become more difficult, frustrating, or frightening than it was a year ago, list what has changed to make you feel that way.

_____

_____

_____

_____

_____

_____

_____

_____

_____

_____

If you have more than a few entries on this list that are serious problems, it may be time to start exploring an alternative living situation.

You Decide Your Living Situation

As we grow older, physical constraints or other factors, coupled with financial changes, may require us to move out of our home. We can lessen the sadness, frustration, and worry over the move by honestly assessing our limitations and talking to family members or to a counselor or other support person from a community agency. But this isn't a decision that should be delegated to our sons and daughters or anyone else.

Living choices range from retirement communities to shared group homes to nursing homes. Remember, it's important that older people live in places that fit their level of functioning. Too much help can be as bad as too little.

Loss of Loved Ones

Though most elderly people have experienced the loss of friends, family, or a spouse, this doesn't mean that each death doesn't begin a grieving process.

People who recognize this and work through the stages of grief, talking about their loss with friends and family, have a greater chance of not

being overwhelmed and paralyzed by grief and sadness. Indeed, talking about our memories and feelings, even the distressing ones, is an excellent way for you to continue finding meaning in life.

Keep a daily or weekly journal in which you make notes about your memories. Who can you share these stories with—children, grandchildren, neighbors, nieces, and nephews? List them here.

_____

_____

_____

_____

_____

Every couple, family, or individual knows some sadness while moving through life's stages. But when we talk to each other about our conflicts, fears, and disappointments as they happen, we find strength we may not have known we possessed.

◆

Think back five or ten or twenty years. Write down your goals from that time regarding the work you do.

_____

_____

_____

_____

Write down the goals you have today.

_____

_____

_____

_____

Have you matured and progressed or merely forgotten those goals?

_____

_____

_____

What can you do to experience greater fulfillment in your work?

_____

_____

_____

EXCEPTIONAL EVENTS AND THE STRESS THAT COMES WITH THEM

Each of us will go through periods of life marked by trouble or sadness or change that seems too great to bear. These may include job loss through downsizing or retirement, the fear of crime that often comes with living in an urban area, divorce, serious illness, and death of a spouse or other loved one. These particular challenges are discussed below, along with suggestions on how to manage the stress that accompanies them.

Job Change

Many of us were raised to believe that we get our self-esteem from the work we do for pay. We focus on money, position, and success at the expense of personal fulfillment. Jean Davis, M.A. Counseling Psychology, is a psychotherapist, career counselor, and outplacement consultant specializing in adult career transitions for more than ten years. In her practice, Davis sees many people who are seeking help because an earlier career choice (usually one made in young adulthood) is no longer viable for them. When they come to her, it's because their "healthy, but reluctant adult wakes up," she says. And that adult starts to give them clues they can't ignore. They may feel something is missing and have a growing sense of imbalance and chaos.

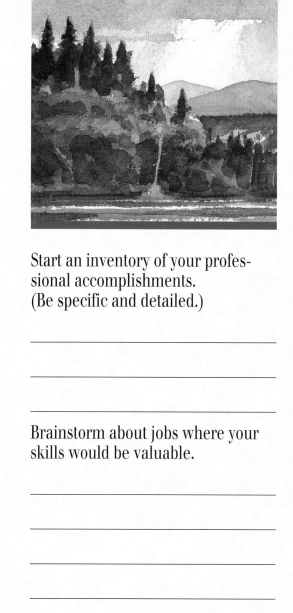

With so many people losing their jobs because of corporate downsizing, Davis also sees more and more people who have lost jobs. One way that she helps them deal with this stress is to demand that they make a

relentless, detailed, personal inventory of their skills and accomplishments on the job. They need this mirror, she says, to acknowledge their strengths and move on to something new.

Davis suggests holding family meetings. This lets the kids know that mom is going back to school so she can get a new job that will be better for her, or that dad is looking for a new job that will make him happier, even though money will be tighter. This way we're passing down to our kids a legacy that emphasizes the importance of meaningful, productive, and rewarding work.

Start an inventory of your professional accomplishments. (Be specific and detailed.)

_____

_____

_____

Brainstorm about jobs where your skills would be valuable.

_____

_____

_____

_____

_____

Who in your family may be changing jobs soon? How can each family member help that person?

_____

_____

_____

_____

_____

_____

Learning to Retire

Our attitude as we approach retirement can be a valuable asset or our biggest obstacle. As with most changes, our perception of the events surrounding retirement will be the most accurate indicator of our emotional health and happiness during the transition. The American Association of Retired Persons (AARP) at 800-424-3410 offers general information about retirement and specific information on services that may be useful to you. You may also want to check with your pastor to see if your church sponsors a retirement group.

The stresses associated with retirement center on the wholesale changes it brings about. These might include changes in financial state, personal habits, residence, responsibilities, and social activities. But while retirement is a *milestone*, it needn't be a *millstone* that weighs you down. Your retirement years can be a chance to contribute more, learn more, make new friends, and truly relax.

This outlook may take time to evolve. Many retirees report that it takes from one to three years to come to an understanding of what their change in work status really means to them. If you are about to retire or have only recently done so, give yourself time to adjust to the change.

Even those who have planned for retirement and look forward to it report that once the initial burst of activity (which may include visits to long-distance family members or a move to a new place) is over, they feel let down. They wake up one day and realize that they don't know what to do next.

Painful as this realization may be, it should be celebrated as a starting point. It offers a chance to discover additional meaning and purpose in life. That may mean volunteering at a local hospital, becoming involved in a senior professional group that provides services for those in need, woodworking, sailing, taking classes at a community college, or group travel. The activity itself is not important, as long as it has meaning for us.

As with any stage in life, in retirement we need a sense of purpose. This is our time to choose—to move toward things that are important to us without the burden of obligation that may have accompanied our job.

Make a list of topics or activities that you've always wanted to learn more about or become involved in.

_____

_____

_____

_____

_____

_____

_____

Concentrate on two of these for a month and then reevaluate to see if you want to continue with them or move on to something else on your list.

What reports and statements can you gather to begin to plan and understand what your monthly balance sheet will look like when you retire?

_____

_____

_____

_____

_____

_____

_____

_____

_____

_____

_____

Contact your AAL District Representative for help in planning.

Start Planning Your Retirement Now

Many people put off thinking about retirement until their working life in offices or factories draws to a close. They often focus on finances as they wonder if they'll have enough money to continue living as they do, worry that they'll be forced to sell their home, or assume they'll have to give up a yearly vacation. Most of these people are surprised and reassured when they finally look at their finances. And others will at least know what they have to do to make their retirement comfortable.

It is never too soon to begin planning for retirement. Prudent financial management can ease many of the fears that are primary causes of stress prior to retirement. It is the anticipation of unpleasantness that keeps most of us from planning ahead. But once we begin the process of planning for retirement, we have an inevitable sense of relief—the stress of anticipating the unpleasantness is over.

The Joys and Challenges of City Living and Country Living

Those of us who live in the city have a special set of daily stressors including smog, crime, noise, traffic, and neighbors above and below us and on either side. But for all the drawbacks, our big cities can be vibrant and healthy places to live. We simply have to recalibrate our stressometers, controlling what we can and accepting what we can't as the price we pay for the convenience, culture, and diversity the city offers.

Those of us who choose to live in the country have other stressors, like inconvenient distances to grocery stores and friends' houses. And Mother Nature is more of a factor. But those same stressors also mean quiet peacefulness and a closeness to the awesome beauty of God's creation.

Almost everyone today, whether living in a city or rural area has an increased fear of crime, particularly violent crime, which seems always on the rise. But whether we live in an apartment building, or a ranch-style home, banding together with our neighbors in "crime stopper" programs or "neighborhood watch groups" is a good way to lower the crime rate and lessen our stress.

What concerns do you have about life in the city or country?

_____

_____

_____

_____

_____

_____

_____

What neighborhood or political organizations could you join to do something about these?

_____

_____

_____

_____

_____

_____

_____

_____

Go to your local library or bookstore and find a book about coping with divorce. Read it as a support in helping you and your children through a difficult process. What advice or insight did you gain from it?

_____

_____

_____

_____

_____

_____

_____

_____

_____

_____

_____

If There's Trouble in Marriage...

Although marriage is intended by God to be lifelong, some marriages do not survive with even the best efforts by a husband and wife.

We should try our best to make our marriage happy and healthy for the sake of ourselves and our children. If we have children, their welfare is naturally a primary concern. But staying together only for the sake of the kids isn't enough for them or for us.

If there is trouble in a marriage, there are ways to strengthen the relationship, like consulting with a marriage counselor or your pastor. There are, however, circumstances in which divorce is appropriate and the only solution.

Even if our marriage was unhappy, the act of changing our living situation can trigger exceptional stress. Expect to feel sadness. It's easy to view ourselves as failures at this time of life. But it's important not to let feelings of guilt keep us away from our church and Christian community. Despite our sinfulness, we *are* forgiven by God. Therefore, we can accept this forgiveness and move on.

Share Your Fears with Your Terminally Ill Loved One

Serious illness often tears a family apart financially and emotionally. Nobody knows what to say or do. Often, nothing is said. But this only serves to isolate and separate the patient and the family members.

By acknowledging that someone we love is dying, we free ourselves to talk to that person about our fears. This also encourages the person to share his or her questions and fears. We don't have to offer answers, just listening helps.

One of the greatest stresses family members and patients feel during a terminal illness is the lack of control that prolonged hospitalization can bring. But a loved one may not have to die in a hospital. Hospice is a special kind of care for dying people that enables them to stay home (or in a hospice center) among their family and friends during the last stages of their illness. The National Hospice Organization at 800-658-8898 can give you more information about hospice care and how you can arrange for it. However, hospice may not be an option in your circumstances.

Try to respect the wishes of your loved one, without bringing yourself to the point of physical or emotional collapse. It won't help your loved one or you.

How can I start a conversation with a loved one who is facing a serious illness?

_____

_____

_____

_____

_____

To whom can I turn if this is more than I can handle?

_____

_____

_____

_____

_____

In what specific ways are you afraid
and sad about the illness or death of
a loved one?

_____

_____

_____

_____

_____

_____

_____

_____

_____

_____

Say these out loud to someone else.

Share Your Grief with Family and Friends

When death does occur, it's particularly important to be patient with yourself and other family members during the time of mourning. It's also important to share your grief with others and not try to contain your feelings and "keep a stiff upper lip." Otherwise, emotions turn inward and can become the basis of a deeper, longer-lasting depression. Expressing our regrets and sorrow to our friends and family can show us we're not alone in wishing we'd done some things differently.

It also may help to join a support group of people who are undergoing similar experiences. Check with your congregation to see if there is a grief support group. Also call the American Cancer Society, 800-227-2345, or your local hospital for referrals to support groups that meet in your area.

Above all,
don't forget to
pray. Prayer
has God's
promise and
tremendous

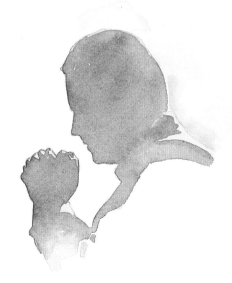

power to comfort and bolster us during a crisis. Invite peace and understanding into your life by thinking about God in everyday places—your kitchen and living room—not just in church on Sundays. (You can read more about prayer on page 62.)

> Compassion is one of the greatest gifts we can give, especially during times of particular trouble. The urge to help others who are suffering is a positive force. We become stronger when we care for each other.
>
> ◆

Think about the death of someone close to you. What did you need from others to help you in your grief?

_____

_____

_____

_____

_____

Make a list of things you could do to help others when they are grieving.

_____

_____

_____

_____

_____

_____

_____

When Someone You Know or Love has a Problem

Addiction and mental illness, especially clinical depression, are two common, serious, and challenging conditions that can confront and tear apart even the closest and most supportive family. In both addiction and mental illness, the afflicted person's friends and family often experience feelings of hopelessness and waste as these diseases reach out to entangle them as well.

When we look only
at what we can do alone,
it's natural to despair.
Our strength comes in
accepting help
from others, especially
from God.

◆

Are you close to someone who has a problem with drugs or alcohol?

_____

_____

_____

_____

List others you could meet with to talk about the problem.

_____

_____

_____

_____

_____

SHARE YOUR CONCERNS ABOUT A FAMILY MEMBER OR FRIEND WHO IS ADDICTED

An alcoholic or chemically dependent family member or friend can easily strain relationships to the point where they snap, leaving us feeling guilty and afraid. We see the serious deterioration in the addicted person, but don't know how to help.

There are things we can do to help the addict. One of the most obvious, but often unexplored, is to sit down with other concerned family members or close friends and share our worries and observations about the addict. This does two things: It reassures us that we are not alone in our fears; and outlines the specific destructive actions the addict is taking.

This informal meeting may also be a good time to consider setting up an intervention for an addicted loved one. The intervention is best led by a mental health professional specifically trained in alcohol and other drug abuse intervention.

This gives family members or friends a chance to try to convince the addict that he or she needs help. During an intervention, participants give the addict specific, detailed accounts of how the addict's abuse of drugs or alcohol has affected them. This lifts the veil of secrecy and denial that often exists in the family. The goal is to get the addict to enter into treatment for the disease.

There are many choices of treatment that we can urge an addict to try. These include Alcoholics Anonymous (AA) or Narcotics Anonymous (NA), detoxification programs, in-patient hospitalization, and individual therapy with a therapist who has a strong background in addictions counseling. The most effective programs will probably include parts of all of these.

Let the Addict Take Responsibility for His or Her Problem

We must understand though, we didn't cause the other person's addiction and we can't cure it. This is especially important to remember when the addicted person is alternately blaming us, pushing us away, and begging us to help. There is a fine line between being supportive and assuming responsibility.

Even if the addict cannot be persuaded to begin a program of recovery, we can gain insight and support by joining Al Anon, or one of the many other support groups for families and friends of addicts. With addiction, actively doing something will probably be better than doing nothing at all.

For information on alcohol or drug treatment centers across the country, call the National Council on Alcoholism and Drug Dependence, 800-622-2255, or the Center for Substance Abuse Treatment, 800-662-4357.

In what ways might you help an addict overcome abuse of drugs or alcohol?

_____

_____

_____

_____

_____

_____

_____

_____

_____

_____

_____

_____

Almost all support groups are free or low cost. Think of a support group that might be helpful to someone you care about.

_____

_____

_____

Look in the yellow pages for a phone number for that group and write it here.

_____

_____

Find a Support Group and Use It in Any Way That's Helpful

No matter what addictions we may have, there is a support group that can help us. Since it was founded in 1935, AA has created a way of approaching addiction that brings people together to share tears, laughter, strength, weakness, frustration, and anger, all the while recovering from their addiction with the help of others who have been there.

More than fifteen million Americans participate in self-help groups, with more than two hundred different groups to choose from. AA, Overeaters Anonymous, Narcotics Anonymous, Cocaine Anonymous, Gamblers Anonymous, Smokers Anonymous, and Sex and Love Addicts Anonymous, are just a few of these. Also, organizations such as the American Anorexia/ Bulimia Association sponsor hundreds of support groups nationwide for those with eating disorders.

In addition, groups such as Al Anon, Alateen, Adult Children of Alcoholics (ACOA), and Gam-Anon function as a means of support for those who are watching loved ones destroy themselves with their addictions.

You may be reluctant to join a group, thinking public disclosure and confession is not for you, but many types of groups exist. If you keep trying, you'll find one that suits you (start your search in your own congregation). When you do, take what you need from it and feel free to ignore advice that doesn't feel right, but keep showing up. Give the support group a chance to work. These groups have a clear record of success in helping people beat addictions and stay true to their recovery.

Successful Therapy Is the Rule

A complication for some people with an addiction problem is mental illness (called "dual diagnosis"). The person with a dual diagnosis needs treatment for both addiction and mental illness. Sobriety won't lead to mental health if another illness is prevalent, and psychological wellness doesn't guarantee sobriety.

We've all heard horror stories about unethical therapists and psychiatric treatment that has left people in worse shape than when they started, but successful therapy is the rule, not the exception.

One of the best ways to find a therapist is to check with a Lutheran social services agency. Or ask your pastor, family and friends. You can also receive advice and a referral to a therapist by calling your city or county mental health association. Your local hospital may also run a mental health clinic. Call there for information.

Don't let lack of money keep you from calling—many programs work on a sliding fee scale, and depending upon income, your family member may be eligible for free services. And some costs might be covered by your health insurance. The National Mental Health Association, 800-433-5959, can also provide referral information.

How do you feel about your therapist or the therapeutic method being used?

_____

_____

_____

_____

_____

_____

If it doesn't feel right, don't end the therapy, but do go to another therapist. You don't have to stay with the same therapist forever when it's not helping.

> We can encourage, support, become angry at, and love the addict, but we can't stop the behavior. Only the addict can do that.
>
> ◆

45

Have you or someone you love experienced five or more of the symptoms of clinical depression for more than two weeks?

_____

_____

_____

_____

List those symptoms here.

_____

_____

_____

_____

_____

_____

_____

_____

_____

_____

Get help now.

CLINICAL DEPRESSION— A COMMON MENTAL ILLNESS

Clinical depression is one of the most serious and common mental illnesses (affecting more than 11 million people every year), but it comes wrapped in layers of misunderstanding and misinformation. It's not a condition you can remedy by simply telling yourself or another person affected to "Snap out of it! It's not so bad."

A depression that lasts more than a couple of weeks and with symptoms that interfere with normal functioning is generally termed "major" or "clinical" depression. It is marked by dramatic and noticeable changes within a person. For example, an outgoing and very social woman who becomes a recluse or a fastidious man who lets his personal appearance and home fall apart, may be showing signs of clinical depression.

Symptoms That Are More than Just the Blues

Clinical depression is more than just feeling sad and blue. It's an illness that disrupts a person's life. It is marked by *persistent* changes in a person's feelings and actions. It calls for treatment that may include psychotherapy, antidepressant medication, or a combination of the two. The most serious complication of depression is the increased risk of suicide. An episode of depression may last for six months or more, but some symptoms can persist for much longer.

The symptoms of clinical depression include loss of energy, loss of interest in things you used to be interested in, sleep disturbance and changes in appetite. Other signs that doctors use to diagnose the disease include: inability to concentrate, restlessness or decreased activity, sadness, feeling hopeless and

worthless, and thoughts of suicide or death. Typically, victims of clinical depression recover and return to their original level of functioning, but many will suffer another episode of depression. Oftentimes, however, their enhanced understanding gained from their first episode enables them to recover more quickly from a subsequent episode of depression.

Matching the Therapy to the Patient

The clinically depressed person can profit from psychotherapy. This "talking therapy" may take different forms. Cognitive therapy helps patients change the way they think, altering their overly pessimistic attitudes. Interpersonal therapy focuses on relationships with others and helps patients relate to people better. Behavioral treatment gives patients a structure to recognize, monitor, and reward their positive actions. Family therapy includes patients' relatives and helps everyone see how their actions affect each other. While some therapists are known for doing a particular kind of therapy, many therapists will match the therapy to the patient, noting which method works best in a particular situation.

Do you have preconceived notions about taking antidepressant medication?

_____

_____

_____

_____

Are you worried about becoming dependent upon it?

_____

_____

_____

Do you see it as an easy answer?

_____

_____

_____

_____

_____

Talk to your therapist about these concerns.

Medication Is Not a Quick-Fix Miracle, but It Can Be a Useful Tool

Another treatment for clinical depression is prescribed medication. Both psychotherapy and medication are effective, but they work best in combination.

Once a person is depressed, there is a chemical within the brain that medication can correct. This medication can often remedy the depression within a short time. However, most patients will take the prescribed drug for four to twelve months. Because there are so many choices of medications, it can be a challenge to find the proper drug and dosage for a particular patient. Drug therapy, or psychopharmacology, is not a quick-fix miracle. It takes time, and the patient must work with the physician to find the most effective medication (that whose side effects interfere least with a person's life).

Help Hotlines

If you or someone you know is suffering from clinical depression and currently not receiving treatment, you should seek help now. Call a Lutheran social service agency (check local listings) or the National Foundation for Depressive Illness at 800-239-1263 for general information and a referral list of doctors who specialize in treating depression. The National Depressive and Manic-Depressive Association at 800-826-3632 also provides infor- mation and can help locate a patient sup- port group near you.

Hopelessness

Few things are more important to mental health than hope. Perhaps the most common and overwhelming symptom of depression is the overall feeling of hopelessness it engenders in those suffering from it. Whatever therapy is used, people suffering from clinical depression need to know that this hopelessness will not disappear overnight. But they also must be continually reassured that even the victims of the severest depressions do recover.

Hope, meaning and purpose in life come with the assurance of God's promises. St. Paul says, "For I am convinced that neither death, nor life, nor angels, nor rulers, nor things present, nor things to come, nor powers, nor height, nor depth, nor anything else in all creation, will be able to separate us from the love of God Christ Jesus our Lord." (Romans 8:38-39). With the assurance of God's promises, people can regain their hopefulness and interest in their work, family, and friends—no matter how bleak their surroundings and spirit may currently seem.

> Clinically depressed people can and do pull through. The darkness doesn't last forever.
>
> ◆

Is a friend or family member who is suffering from clinical depression trying to push you away?

_____

_____

_____

_____

_____

Try not to take it personally, and do keep in close contact anyway. Who can you talk to if you feel worried about this?

_____

_____

_____

_____

_____

_____

_____

_____

50

Finding
Spiritual
Harmony

God is the source of all harmony. The key to increasing harmony of mind, body, and spirit is in our relationship to God, because it is from the harmony of this relationship that we will discover harmony with nature, with other people, and with ourselves.

Scientists are just beginning to recognize the amazing harmony of mind, body, and spirit that is built into God's ordering of creation. How ironic that scientists know more about discrete functions of mind and body than has ever been known in the history of the world but have only recently uncovered evidence for what some primitive cultures have always known: *that mind and body are a harmonious whole.*

In harmony
with God, we receive
the gifts of peace,
wholeness, and
eternal rest.

◆

THE MIND-BODY CONNECTION AND SPIRITUALITY

There are many everyday examples of how the mind influences the body. For instance, many of us blush when embarrassed or when we're self-consciously pleased. *Feelings* produce this warm red flush. Or consider how some of us can't control our shaking knees, chattering teeth, and fluttering voices when we have to speak to a crowd.

Physicians have always known that illness and death are a serious threat to widows and widowers in the year following the death of their spouse, but they couldn't tell you why. Now we know at least one of the factors. Recent studies show that social support is a primary factor in maintaining health. A person who has had a heart attack is fifty percent more likely to have a second heart attack within six months if he or she is living alone. Persons without social support are more vulnerable to every life-threatening disease. Some studies show that decreased immune efficiency is one of the major causes, but whatever the cause it's clearly linked to a spiritual experience of grieving, loneliness, and hopelessness. And, as Christians, we know that it's not just social support, but God's presence mediated through others, that sustains us in our experiences of loss and helplessness.

It's probably not coincidental that these discoveries of science have been accompanied by a deepening interest in spirituality in our country. There is a hunger for spiritual growth among people who recognize that the answer to stress, depression, and the increasing number of life-style diseases is not medication but increased harmony of mind, body, and spirit.

The popularity of authors like Bernie Siegel is evidence of the wide-spread interest in discovering ways to deepen spirituality and increase the harmony of mind and body. In his best-selling book *Love, Medicine & Miracles,* Siegel writes, "...The state of the mind changes the state of the body by working through the central nervous system, the endocrine system, and the immune system. Peace of mind sends the body a 'live' message, while depression, fear, and unresolved conflict give it a 'die' message."

In Harmony with God

Spirituality is the turf of religion rather than medicine, and Christians rightly turn to the church and their pastor in spiritual matters to be sure that their spirituality is firmly grounded in Christ.

We can benefit from such simple, natural ways as laughter to increase the harmony of mind and body. But deeper spiritual needs call for something more. As St. Augustine said, "Our hearts are restless until they rest in Thee." Harmony in relation to God must be the grounding for increasing harmony of mind and body. That harmony we find in Christ, from whom we receive the gifts of forgiveness, peace, wholeness and eternal rest.

Our best guide to increasing the harmony of mind and body will not be found in the spiritual gurus who are promoting the latest self-help techniques in publications, workshops, and television appearances. We need not dismiss the wisdom and experience of some of these spiritual guides, but we should be aware of the need for discernment and the importance of grounding all spirituality in Christ.

For example, most of the New Age spirituality that promises increased harmony of mind and body is rooted in Eastern philosophy and religion. The age-old spiritual disciplines of Christianity, such as meditation and prayer, are surer guides as we look for ways to deepen our relationship to Christ, the one true source of harmony at every level of creation.

Maintaining a Spiritual, Physical, and Intellectual Balance

Most of us will readily admit that we lack balance in our lives and feel a lack of harmony as a result of it. The stress that we feel is a symptom of imbalance. Too many things to do; too little time to do them all. Too many demands from job, parents, children, and church; too little energy to meet them all. It's not enough to "just say no," though we know the need to set limits.

We also need to ask for forgiveness, because the greatest cause of imbalance in our lives is sin and the greatest source of harmony is a restored relationship to God through Christ. So how do we find balance and harmony in a life that is inevitably stressful because of our overburdened lifestyles?

Physical Exercise

Media messages bombard us with encouragement to be more physically active. Join an exercise class. Swim. Jog or walk. It's good advice. You'll feel better if you do. Your stress level will drop. Your health will improve. And you will feel more in tune with your body than you have for a long time. It's easy to think that harmony of mind and body is dependent more on mind than body, but anybody who has experienced the "high" that comes with the release of endorphins after a good workout knows it's often the other way around. Physical exercise brings balance and harmony to our lives.

You can easily add a spiritual component to many forms of exercise. For example, as you jog or do other aerobic exercise alternate words or phrases as prayers with each breath you take, such as "Breath of Life," "Breath of God," or "Praise God," "Thank God." You can transform your daily walk into what Flora Wuellner calls "a parable walk," in which you look for signs of God's presence in the surrounding world of nature and contemplate the goodness of God's creation.

Intellectual Stimulation

We also need intellectual stimulation for a balanced life. We all have a natural desire to learn.

What phrase from Scripture or hymn is particularly meaningful to you (for example, "Be still, my soul")?

_____

_____

_____

_____

_____

_____

_____

Make the phrase a breath prayer, speaking the words each time you exhale. Do that for two minutes the first time, and then extend the time gradually to five minutes.

Years ago, intellectual activity was defined more in terms of *remembering*. During those years, many educators believed that the goal of education was to memorize all there was to know. Consistent with this, Christians memorized scripture passages and hymn verses and could later recite them or recall them to think about their meaning.

The information explosion of today has shifted the emphasis from memorization to *how to organize and retrieve information* so we can use it to solve problems. With the shift from memorization to organization and retrieval, something was lost.

Another valuable form of intellectual activity that is less known today (or at least relegated to a "gifted few") is imagination. Many adults seem to think that God gave us imagination to use only in childhood. It seems all right for a few adults like poets and musicians to use their imaginations, but for most of us in the work-a-day world, imagination is better left alone. Perhaps some adults are afraid to use imagination because it is here especially that the intellectual and the spiritual meet.

Imagination can draw us into the heart of spiritual meaning and intellectual stimulation. Awaken the imagination for a deeper-than-intellectual experience by reading or listening to a powerful story, such as the parables of Jesus, to reflect on the meaning of life. Scripture, especially the Old Testament, is full of word pictures. When we "picture" God's activity among us, He becomes more real to us. When we "see" what God is doing in our lives and in our world, we are better able to find meaning in our everyday life.

There are many ways to stimulate the intellect that help us reflect deeply on the meaning of our lives as Christians and help us find balance and harmony in life. It might be as simple as working a crossword puzzle or as profound as composing an essay on spiritual truths. You could take a course in music appreciation or comparative religions at your local community college. Or make up a story to tell your children or grandchildren. You and your spouse or friend could read the same book or article and discuss it. You could memorize a section of Scripture or a hymn, and probe the meaning for your life and faith.

Spiritual Nurture

Our world values intellectual stimulation for its own sake, but separates it from spiritual nurture. That's an odd division. Scripture speaks of being "spiritually minded," bringing together the intellectual and the spiritual. Spiritually minded people use their minds for more than self-satisfying or self-serving purposes. Their spirit of exploration and curiosity is enriched by the question: "How can this learning be applied for the greater good of others?" Spiritual includes that which is religious, of course, but it has a much broader meaning.

Although we all have spiritual needs, not everyone turns to religion to meet those needs. We all need hope, love, forgiveness, and some purpose for living, but not everyone finds the ultimate fulfillment of those needs in relation to God. Christians do. The spiritual domain is central to life for Christians, and the source of an indestructible peace of mind. That's why spiritual discipline is so central to the Christian life and why we focus particular attention upon it in the sections to follow.

Peace of Mind
Through Spiritual Hope

Hope is an expectant leaning into the future. Hope is rooted in and sustained by promises, apart from which it will wither and die. People die without hope—literally.

Feelings of helplessness and hopelessness trigger a paralysis that deadens both mind and body. The phenomenon is most dramatically seen in animal studies. Dogs that are placed in a position of inescapable shock will eventually make no attempt to escape the shock even if there is opportunity to do so. A mouse that is placed in a jar filled with water will soon die through a slowing of respiration and heartbeat, and that will happen even more quickly if the whiskers by which it orients itself to its surroundings are cut. But if a mouse is placed in a jar of water and then removed, and this is done repeatedly, it will swim for long periods of time without any evidence of giving up or dying.

The same is true for people. Physicians despair when their patients no longer have the will to live, because their best work will not save them. But cancer patients, for instance, who refuse to accept a terminal prognosis and continue to have hope, live longer than patients who passively accept the inevitable.

There is no substitute for the peace of mind that comes through hope. People of hope are people with positive attitudes. They are the people who live longer after a diagnosis of terminal cancer. They are the hardy people who are less likely to become ill. There is a direct correlation between positive, hopeful people and health.

But hope is fleeting if it's not grounded in Christ. Every other hope is threatened by the circumstances of life, when we die if not before. The most powerful biblical illustration of that is the story of Jesus about the rich man who had placed his hope in the abundance of goods he had gathered, a hope that vanished when he was told he would die that very night (Luke 12:16-21). Contrast that with the enduring hope that nothing can separate us from the love of God, as stated in Romans 8:38-39 and quoted on the last page of Section III of this book. The peace of mind that accompanies this assurance is indestructible, no matter what stresses and distresses life may bring.

There is no deeper yearning than the yearning for spiritual hope and the peace of mind it brings. The loving and healing presence of Christ is our spiritual hope. That presence is felt in many ways all of the time, but we are most likely to experience it when we are gathered with others around Word and Sacrament, the means of grace. Worship is central for nurturing spiritual hope. But there is also a personal spiritual path that we can follow. Meditation and prayer are inward disciplines that open the door to the presence of God and lead us beyond surface living into the depths.

How much time do you spend reflecting on your inner life? Most of the time our attention is focused on what is happening outside of us rather than in the center of our self, even in church. Many of us are pragmatic doers, spending most of our waking hours in task-oriented activities. If you spend very little time with your inner life, you may want to spend more time in meditation and prayer, proven methods for cultivating the inner life and deepening spiritual hope.

When is the best time of day for you to spend alone in meditation and prayer?

_____

_____

_____

Where is a quiet place for this time?

_____

_____

_____

There is no substitute for the hope that comes to us through our faith. Prescribed medications and all the possessions in the world won't replace it.

◆

Close your eyes so that you won't be distracted by anything in your surroundings. In your mind's eye go deep within yourself and create a room there. You can furnish it however you wish, but make it a place that invites quiet reflection, perhaps with a large picture window overlooking a lake or a mountain landscape. This is a room for you and you alone, and others may enter only by invitation.

Picture Jesus standing at the door and knocking (Rev. 3:20). He is there, not forcing his presence on you, but ready and eager to spend some time with you. Imagine what would happen from this point on, letting the experience unfold naturally without any expectation of specific outcomes. Describe the experience here:

_____

_____

_____

_____

_____

_____

_____

Practicing Meditation

Richard Foster says that "if we hope to move beyond the superficialities of our culture, including our religious culture, we must be willing to go down into the recreating silences, into the inner world of contemplation" (*The Celebration of Discipline*, S.F.: HarperCollins, 1978, p. 15). The practice of meditation is as ancient as the human race. "Isaac went out to meditate in the field in the evening" (Gen. 24:63). Jesus made a habit of withdrawing to "a deserted place by himself" (Matt 14:13) for prayer and meditation.

The purpose of meditation is to create a spiritual space within, an inner sanctuary of the heart where Christ is present. It's through the word of God and the sacraments that Christ enters our heart, but the imagination is a wonderful tool for enhancing the experience of his presence.

Of all the wonderful gifts that God showered on us in creation, our imagination is probably the most under used. Lively and creative in children, the imagination gets dulled and deadened in an educational system that stresses objectivity and detachment. And some fear that

the imagination is untrustworthy and can be used by Satan. It's true that the imagination, like all our faculties, operates under the conditions of a fallen humanity, but God can sanctify our imagination as well as our heart and reason. All our faculties can mediate his presence as we worship and meditate on his word.

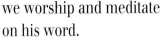

The Interfaith Health Program at The Carter Center of Emory University is a national information clearinghouse for health-related issues for faith groups. Dr. Thomas Droege, associate director of the center, has studied the spiritual aspects of mind-body connection extensively. In his book, *The Healing Presence* (S.F.: HarperCollins, 1992), Droege offers meditation and guided imagery exercises that are designed for purposes of meditation.

According to Droege, guided imagery is a deeper-than-intellectual way of making the stories of and about Jesus come alive in our imagination. The use of imagery is a method for making scenes, memories, and stories more vivid and closer to experience than abstract thought. What makes a good story so powerful is that you can picture the events being described and feel like you are part of the action. Jesus was a master at this. "A sower

What can you do to enliven your prayer life?

_____

_____

_____

_____

After trying one of these ways, note its effect:

_____

_____

_____

_____

went out to sow his seed," and we picture a man with a sackful of seed in a field that has just been plowed.

Guided imagery is certainly not the only form of meditation, though the use of imagery is common in all forms of meditation. The central form of meditation for all the devotional masters is reflection upon Scripture. The goal is to deepen experience, not broaden knowledge. The method of meditation is not so much to study the passage, understand the context, and think about its theological implications, but to deepen one's experience of the presence of God.

Take the statement of Jesus, "My peace I give to you" (John 14:27). The purpose is not to define peace but rather to experience and enter into the peace and forgiveness that comes with Christ's presence in our lives. The body relaxes, the mind awakens, and the spirit is energized by a peace which passes understanding.

Prayer

Meditation introduces us to the inner life, but it is prayer that carries us into the very heart of God. To be carried into the heart of God is to see things from God's point of view, "to think God's thoughts after him: to desire the things he desires, to love the things he loves, to will the things he wills" (*Celebration of Discipline*, p. 33). That's why praying is more listening than talking, more a matter of being sensitively attuned to the presence and activity of God than it is petitioning God to make changes in our lives that fit our limited perspective.

God is in control and in a better position than we are to chart the course of things. That's the first principle of prayer. The second is that prayer changes things,

especially the one who prays. Don't pray unless you're ready to be transformed and see the world transformed. Don't be too quick to pray "if it be your will" as a qualification of your prayer. Instead be tuned in to God's will, about which we know much from Scripture, and then pray with expectant trust that it will be realized. Prayer is powerful stuff. Never underestimate it.

Prayer is both natural and learned. It is as natural as a child going to his or her father or mother. That's why Jesus encourages us to say "Our Father" and to call God "Abba." Children don't hesitate to ask their parents for anything if their trust is based on fulfilled promises. Their requests are not always answered, nor should they be. What's important is the relationship: trust, open communications, loyalty, faithfulness. When our relationship to God has those qualities, prayer is as natural and spontaneous as the beating of our heart.

But we also need to learn to pray, just as the disciples did. There are many books of prayer and about prayer. You no doubt have some in your possession. They are useful tools for focusing attention on matters we may forget and lending us words that express our thoughts and feelings in ways that seem just right. A spiritual guide can also be helpful, perhaps your pastor or maybe a good friend who would be willing to share experiences with you. Attending a retreat is an excellent way to learn more about prayer, share experiences with others, and deepen your prayer life. The following suggestions may help.

A good way to keep your prayer life fresh is to try new things, in much the same way that you would in any relationship that is important to you. Keep what is

Picture a place that is sacred for you, perhaps a church or some natural setting that you treasure. Imagine that Jesus is there, and you are engaging him in a discussion of a matter of great importance to you. Record the ensuing dialogue, both what Jesus says and what you say, letting the conversation flow naturally and spontaneously:

_____

_____

_____

_____

Take a nature walk, no more than ten minutes the first time, in a place that is quiet and secluded. Experience the wonder of God's creation and the power of his presence. What did you learn by the experience?

_____

_____

_____

_____

_____

_____

In prayer, listening is more important than talking. Be sensitively attuned to the presence of God and his message to you.

◆

working well, but look for new ways to deepen and enliven your prayer life.

One of the effects of a deepened prayer life is an increase of the harmony of mind and body, and that's one way to measure the health of your prayer life. That's not the only reason for praying of course, and those who pray just to feel more at peace with themselves and God may be shocked when they discover that God is calling them to a life of service and sacrifice that they see mirrored in the one to whom they are praying.

Making Yourself Happy by Helping Others

The reason for praying and helping others is not just to make us feel better. If that's our primary motivation, we are putting ourselves rather than God at the center of life. That's always been the primal sin of humanity, beginning with Adam and Eve. Feeling happy and at peace with ourselves and God are evidence of health, but as Christians we know that health is not an end in itself.

We help others because they are in need. It's as simple as that. We do it for their sakes, and the benefits we receive are blessings of God that accompany the fulfillment of our humanity. It's an unexplainable process—a paradox—that giving of ourselves brings so much more to us in return.

True helpers don't discriminate in their response to need. They don't see color, race, gender, or age. They see need. And they respond to need as naturally and spontaneously as did Jesus, not out of duty but out of love. That's why you never have to talk a true helper into helping.

Duty is never a primary motivation in a true helper, and neither is guilt. Have you ever noticed the attitude of duty-bound helpers? It's generally a grim "let's get it over with" attitude, at least in the beginning, though often helping others generates feelings that transform the duty into genuine service.

Helping often calls for sacrifice. How can that make you happy? The question is prompted by the idea that sacrifice means giving up something rather than liberating us from something. The basic meaning of sacrifice is "to make holy." In this sense, sacrifice means giving up something that keeps us from being holy or whole. It means letting go of anything that keeps us from belonging wholly to God.

Love always implies sacrifice, because love looks to the good of another. It is in letting go of ourselves that we discover our relationships with others, and through letting go, we grow into a deeper experience of love and life. What could bring more happiness than that?

Offer hope to someone by doing simple things. You can offer to run an errand for an elderly neighbor or give up your seat on a crowded rush-hour bus to someone who looks even more exhausted than you feel. What can you think of to help someone else today?

_____

_____

_____

_____

The happiness you feel is directly proportional to the amount of helpfulness you offer to others.

CONCLUSION: A PLAN FOR LIVING

As you consider your personal well-being, you might discover how much you've yet to learn about yourself and others. This realization need not be discouraging, but is actually reason for *celebration*. It's a reminder of your need and capacity to improve and cultivate your physical, emotional, and spiritual health.

The fine but firm connections between these three components of your personal well-being become more clear as you begin to pay attention to them. Strengthening them prepares you to accept the gift of harmony of mind, body and spirit that God wants for us all.

It's impossible to completely separate these aspects of personal well-being—they don't work independently of each other. Take, for instance, the sensations you might experience as you hike a wooded path. First, you experience the physical exertion—your pulse rate increases, your calf muscles stretch—you begin to feel looser and stronger. Then you walk farther and you hear yourself becoming quieter. You shed some of your worries. You become less tense. You walk farther still and you become aware of the natural beauty and harmony around you. You find yourself comforted by this reminder of God's presence in your life. You feel at ease and at peace.

The walk, the improved frame of mind, the heightened sense of the presence of God—each happening in relation to the other. You are taking an active step to make them happen. And you don't have to be in a natural setting to see and feel these connections. You might feel the connection as you begin to follow a healthy eating plan: As a result, you find you have more energy to

expend on your family or friends, which in turn fills you with the joy of giving to and doing for others.

Of course, we can't expect a harmony of body, mind and spirit to be readily available just because we need it in a crisis situation. As with anything, practice makes perfect—when we take an active, daily role in promoting our personal well-being, we prepare ourselves for a fuller future. While external stressors will always exist, by becoming physically, emotionally, and spiritually healthy we can ensure that our response to the stress in our lives is measured and appropriate.

This book offered guidelines to help you through some of the problems that almost everyone faces at some time in life. Refer back to its pages often—particularly those where you've recorded your thoughts. And use those thoughts as a basis to create a plan for living life the way it was meant to be lived: fully, with a sense of perspective about the things that somehow don't seem right, and a deep appreciation for the many things that do.

WHO TO CONTACT FOR HELP

American Association
of Retired Persons (AARP)   1-800-424-3410

American Cancer Society   1-800-227-2345

Center for Substance
Abuse Treatment   1-800-662-4357

Lutheran Social Services of your state
(see local telephone directory).

National Council on Alcoholism
and Drug Dependence   1-800-622-2255

National Depressive and
Manic-Depressive Association   1-800-826-3632

National Foundation for
Depressive Illness   1-800-239-1263

National Hospice Organization   1-800-658-8898

National Mental Health Association   1-800-433-5959

Wisconsin Lutheran Child and
Family Service. Headquarters: 1-414-353-5000

BIBLIOGRAPHY

Antonovsky, Aaron. *Unraveling the Mystery of Health: How People Manage Stress & Stay Well.* San Francisco: Jossey-Bass Publications, 1987.

Arbetter, Sandra. "Handling Stress," *Current Health.* October 1992.

Bakken, Kenneth. *Call to Wholeness.* New York: Crossroads, 1985.

Bakken, Kenneth. *Journey Toward Wholeness.* New York: E.P. Dutton, 1988.

Buckman, Robert. *I Don't Know What to Say...* New York: Vintage Books, 1992.

Chaitow, Leon. *The Stress Protection Plan.* Hammersmith, London: Thorsons, 1992.

Charlesworth, Ph.D., Edward A. and Nathan, Ph.D., Ronald G. *Stress Management: A Comprehensive Guide to Wellness.* New York: Atheneum, 1984.

Cousins, Norman. *Head First: The Biology of Hope.* New York: E.P. Dutton, 1989.

Davis, Jean. Interview with author, 7/25/93.

Droege, Ph.D., Thomas. *The Faith Factor in Healing.* San Francisco: HarperCollins, 1991.

Droege, Ph.D., Thomas. *The Healing Presence.* San Francisco: HarperCollins, 1992.

Foster, Richard. *Celebration of Discipline*. San Francisco: HarperCollins, 1988.

Frank, Arthur. *At the Will of the Body*. Boston: Houghton Mifflin, 1991.

Galanter, Marc. "The End of Addiction," *Psychology Today*. November/December, 1992.

Hales, Dianne. *Depression: Psychological Disorders and Their Treatment*. New York, Philadelphia: Chelsea House Publishers, 1989.

Hirschfeld, M.D., Robert. *When the Blues Won't Go Away*. New York: Macmillan, 1991.

Leman, Kevin. *Keeping Your Family Together when the World Is Falling Apart*. New York: Delacorte Press, 1992.

Levy, Michael T. *Parenting Mom & Dad*. New York: Prentice Hall, 1991.

Mairs, Nancy. *Ordinary Time: Cycles in Marriage, Faith, and Renewal*. Boston: Beacon Press, 1993.

Marano, Hara Estroff. "The Reinvention of Marriage," *Psychology Today*. January/February, 1992.

Myers, David G. "The Secrets of Happiness," *Psychology Today*. July/August, 1992.

National Hospice Organization. Brochure — "Hospice: A Special Kind of Caring." Arlington, Virginia.

National Mental Health Association. Brochure —
"Answers to Your Questions About Clinical Depression."
Alexandria, Virginia.

O'Neill, Molly. "Unusual Heart Therapy Wins Coverage
from Large Insurer," *New York Times.* 7/28/93.

Ornstein, Robert & Sobel, David. *The Healing Brain.* New
York: Simon & Schuster, 1987.

Peterson, Linda. "Teen Rebellion: The Good, the Bad,
and the Healthy," *Redbook.* January, 1992

Peterson, Susan. "Insomnia?" *Chicago Tribune.* 7/18/93.

Picard, Frank L. *Family Intervention.* Hillsboro, Oregon:
Beyond Words Publishing, Inc., 1989.

Register, Cheri. *Living with Chronic Illness.* New York:
Bantam Books, 1989.

"Removing Obstacles to Altruism." *Modern Maturity.*
Oct/Nov 1993.

Roesch, Roberta. *The Encyclopedia of Depression.* New
York: Facts on File, 1991.

Seward, Brian. "Spiritual Well-being: A Health Education
Model," *Journal of Health Education.* May/June, 1991.
Vol. 22, No. 3.

Schmidt, Stephen. *Living with Chronic Illness.*
Minneapolis: Augsburg, 1989.

Siegel, Bernie S. *Love, Medicine & Miracles.* New York: Harper & Row, 1988.

Selye, Hans. "History and Present Status of the Stress Concept." in *Stress and Coping: An Anthology,* Alan Monat and Richard S. Lazarus, eds. New York: Columbia University Press, 1991.

Styron, William. *Darkness Visible: A Memoir of Madness.* New York: Random House, 1990.

Veninga, Robert L. *Your Renaissance Years: Making Retirement the Best Years of Your Life.* Boston: Little, Brown & Company, 1991.

Walsh, Froma. "Loss," *Psychology Today.* July/August, 1992.

Weinstein, Grace W. *Life Plans: Looking Forward to Retirement.* New York: Holt, Rinehart and Winston, 1979.

Wilson, Jan R. and Judy. *Addictionary.* New York: Simon & Schuster, 1992

Wuellner, Flora Slosson. *Heart of Healing, Heart of Light.* Nashville: The Upper Room, 1985.

Wuellner, Flora Slosson. *Prayer & Our Bodies.* Nashville: The Upper Room, 1985.

Wuellner, Flora Slosson. *Prayer, Stress, & Our Inner Wounds.* Nashville: The Upper Room, 1985.

NOTES

NOTES

NOTES

NOTES

NOTES

NOTES